Boxer's Shorts 5

More Than Just A Brief Attempt At Humor

THE SPORTS BOOK

Punchline Press
Wilmette, Illinois

CREATED BY ROBERT BOXER M.D.
ILLUSTRATED BY DARNELL TOWNS

Manuscript Editor
Susan Cherry

Book and Cover Design
Darnell Towns/Robert Boxer

Typesetting and Production Services
Sans Serif, Inc.

Cover Illustration
Darnell Towns

Back Cover Photograph
Self-Timer

Back Cover Background Art Design
Darnell Towns

Published by Punchline Press
P.O. Box 308, Wilmette, Illinois 60091

Printed in the United States of America

First Edition, October, 2006

Library of Congress Catalog Number 2006931173
ISBN 13: 978-0-9620687-4-4
ISBN 10: 0-9620687-4-8

Contents

Dedications

To my sons, Stephen and Richard, for sharing my lifelong interest in and appreciation of sports.

To the memory of the late Larry Soibel, father of my daughter-in-law Lisa. Larry was a devoted husband and father and the most dedicated grandfather I can imagine. His unselfish love, attention, and affection for his grandchildren will forever be remembered. Larry was also an ardent sports lover and a lifelong Chicago Bears fan. He had season tickets for many years and attended games in even the coldest weather.

This book is also dedicated to professional and amateur athletes of all ages and to everyone who enjoys participating in and/or watching sports.

Illustrator's Dedication

What can I say? God gave me this incredible ability long before I knew what I was doing. I thank God for that. If I didn't know how to draw, I'd probably be in the movies somewhere trying to upstage Sidney Poitier, with little success. Lots and lots and lots of love to my family because they would support me even if I were on the street corner drawing cartoons of people as they walked past trying to avoid me. Just for the record, I've never done that.

Foreword

I have known Bob Boxer for more than 30 years. Until I read *BOXER'S SHORTS (More Than Just a Brief Attempt at Humor),* I thought Bob was a well-grounded, sensible person. After reading all four books, I have come to realize that he is closer to insane than normal. Fortunately, his off-the-wall mind has produced some of the funniest material I have ever seen. Anyone reading *BOXER'S SHORTS 5* will have a perpetual smile.

Jerry Reinsdorf
Chairman, Chicago White Sox/Chicago Bulls

Preface

My fifth book of original pun cartoons is about sports. It is brilliantly illustrated by Darnell Towns, who did the drawings for my previous books and conceived the cartoon on page 216 and contributed to the cartoon on page 162. Since sports have universal appeal, *Boxer's Shorts 5* is intended for people of all ages and walks of life. Chicago is a fantastic sports town. We are fortunate to have two major-league baseball teams. The Windy City is also home to professional basketball, football, hockey, soccer, arena football, horse and auto racing, golf, tennis, great college football and basketball—and more!

Sports are fun and help us keep in shape, often in a social setting. They teach us how to unselfishly work with others as both a leader and a follower. Sports foster discipline by requiring us to follow the coach, manager, or team captain in both the game pattern and individual plays. In addition, sports develop character, build and maintain friendships, and teach life lessons. Success in sports can contribute to self-esteem and confidence. Spectator sports foster pride, appreciation of excellence, and social interaction, and provide diversion, entertainment and enjoyment

I would like to congratulate The Chicago White Sox for the incredible excitement and pride they created with their victorious 2005 season and sweep of the World Series. I also wish to congratulate the Chicago Rush for winning the 2006 Arena Football League Championship after only six years in the league. In addition, I would like to welcome to Chicago the energetic, athletic,

and exciting Chicago Sky of the Women's National Basketball Association. I also wish the Chicago Fire much success in their new home, Toyota Park in Bridgeview. Those of us who are old enough to remember the Chicago Bears' Super Bowl win in 1985, and the six Chicago Bulls NBA Championships in the nineties, look forward to sharing that excitement and pride again.

Boxer's Shorts 5 incorporates several cartoons from the first four books in the series, as well as cartoons that appeared in *THE MAIN EVENT, Monthly Sports Journal for Physicians*. Our cartoons were in that monthly publication for four years.

BASEBALL

THE SOX PLAYING THE ORIOLES.

SPRING TRAINING

"THE MANAGER'S BRINGING IN A RELIEF PITCHER FROM THE BULL PEN."

"SWING AND A MISS."

"Now watch this Tu Tu Pitch."

".....striking out with two out in the bottom of the ninth and the bases loaded. Now do you understand what a Cardinal sin is?"

"You do know that you're being charged with HIT AND RUN!"

"I can see that this game will have a lot of Full Counts".

"She had perfect pitch and I want you to do the same."

"You can bet that with men on base, when Abraham comes up to bat...he'll sacrifice".

A FOWL TIP.

Baseball, a game of inches.

"DON'T YOU KNOW ABOUT THE INFIELD FLY RULE?"

"THE MANAGER IS BRINGING IN A RELIEF PITCHER."

"I LOVE THE IDEA OF NAMING YOUR SON HOMER."

CLOTHES LINE SINGLE.

"Well, the guy is a baseball manager, he could always use another PITCHER."

23

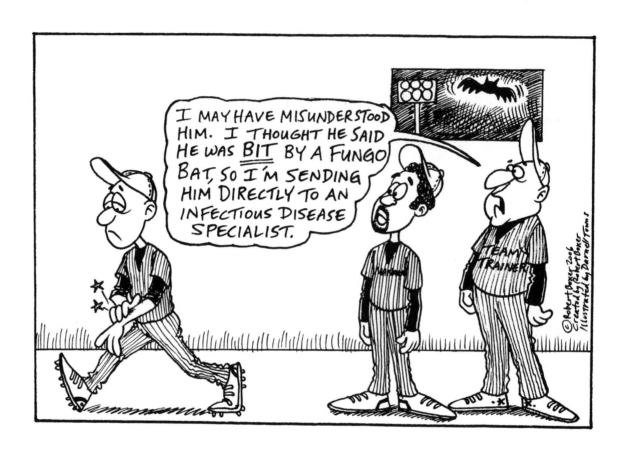

"Somebody said that there was an opening at first base".

ONE BALL, ONE STRIKE.

"The Batboy is sick, so his Dad is filling in".

"20,000 LEAGUES UNDER THE SEA."

"They really brought him up from the minors".

"Hazel, I think you've got to learn more about sports."

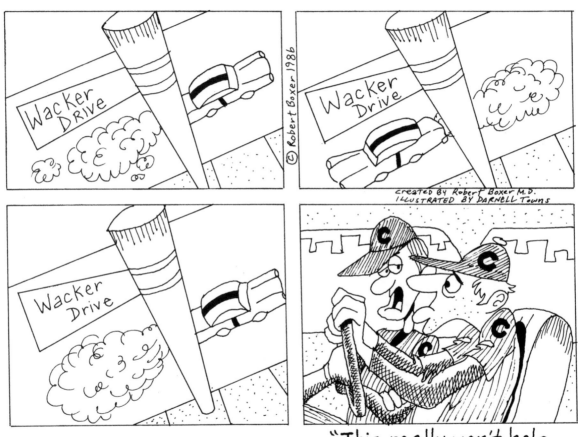

"This really won't help your hitting."

A FOWL BALL

"WHAT A COINCIDENCE, WE WERE JUST YESTERDAY DISCUSSING "CORN ON THE COBB.""

THROWN OUT STEALING 2ND BASS.

"HANK IS NOTORIOUS FOR WALKING IN RUNS."

"HE WAS REALLY IMPRESSED IN SCHOOL WITH THE OTTOMAN EMPIRE."

"I THOUGHT WHEN I BOUGHT THIS TEAM FOR THAT LOW PRICE THERE WOULD BE A CATCH SOMEWHERE."

"YOU CAN ONLY PICKET IN THIS AREA."

Jim has always wanted to manage in the minors.
© Robert Boxer 1988
created by Robert Boxer
illustrated by Darrell Towns

"I DON'T HAVE ANY CARDS LEFT TO PLAY."

43

"WELL, I DON'T KNOW YOU GUYS THAT WELL, BUT WE'RE GOING TO HAVE AT LEAST THREE HOMERS IN EVERY GAME."

44

"WHAT ARE WE GOING TO DO WITH ALL OF THESE ILLEGALLY PARKED FANS?"

"You Do Know that we now have `Lites' at Wrigley Field."

47

"BARRY BONDS IS ONE OF VERY FEW PLAYERS WHO CAN HIT A SINKING LINER FOR A HOME RUN."

"HE THOUGHT THE ROSTER WAS DUE FOR **TRIMMING.**"

50

"I KNEW THIS NEW PLAYER WOULD SHOW US SOME INTERESTING BUNTING."

"NOBODY WILL GET TO FIRST BASE WITH HER."

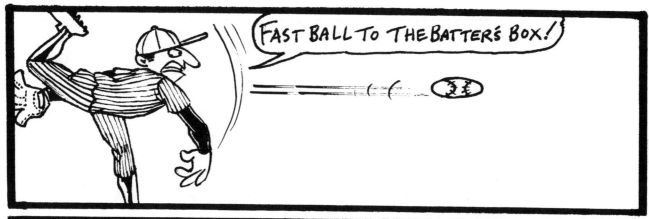

TOP OF THE FIFTH.   BOTTOM OF THE FIFTH

56

"THE LAST CHANCE BATTER STRUCK OUT. IS HE MR. OCTOBER OR WAS HE JUST THE FALL GUY?"

"The Pitching coach is especially interested
in Larkin with his unusual wind-up".

"Broken Bat Single."

"WHEN HE WAS PLAYING PROFESSIONAL BASEBALL HE WAS A GREAT PITCHER. IN FACT HE'S STILL A GREAT CLOSER."

FOOTBALL

63

"OH, I DIDN'T EXPECT CHRIS. THE TRAINER TOLD ME THAT HE HAD A **HIP POINTER**."

"DON'T WORRY, DR. SMITH IS VERY GOOD. HE PLAYED PROFESSIONAL FOOTBALL. HE WAS A PULLING GUARD."

65

"DOESN'T THAT TIP OFF THE OTHER TEAM THAT IT'S GOING TO BE A QUARTERBACK SNEAK?"

"NOW WE KNOW WHO THE SLOT RECEIVER IS."

"DOES THIS MEAN THAT THE NEXT PLAY IS GOING TO BE A QUARTERBACK DRAW?"

"MAYBE THE QUARTERBACK IS TRYING TO DRAW THE OTHER TEAM OFFSIDES."

"DOESN'T THAT TIP OFF THE OTHER TEAM THAT IT'S GOING TO BE A CROSSING PATTERN?"

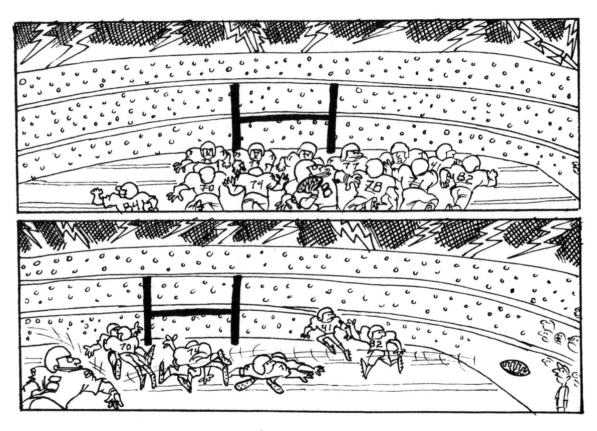

"THIS IS ONE INSTANCE WHERE 'INTENTIONAL GROUNDING' IS A VERY SMART MOVE."

"HE'S PICKING UP THESE HOMELESS GUYS BECAUSE HE'S PLANNING TO RUN A LOT OF 'DOWN AND OUT' PATTERNS."

73

"THANK GOODNESS WE HAVE A GENUINE LONG SNAPPER."

"DON'T WORRY ABOUT MAKING CHANGE FOR THE COACH.
HE'LL BE HAPPY IF YOU JUST GIVE HIM A QUARTERBACK."

THE TEAM HAS RESPONDED WELL TO AN OLDER COACH
WHO'S DEFINITELY PATERNO.

"HE'S ALSO THE FIRST STRING QUARTERBACK."

"BOY, YOU KNOW HE'S LOYAL TO HIS POSITION ON THE TEAM."

"It's obvious to the defense and us that the Quarter-back intends to throw the BOMB"!

"Of all the post-season bowl games, the hardest on the players is this 'Punch Bowl'."

82

"I UNDERSTAND THAT SINCE HE WAS IN THE ARMY, HE SHOWS UP DRESSED THAT WAY AT VETERAN'S STADIUM IN PHILADELPHIA AND SOLDIER FIELD IN CHICAGO."

83

"HONEY, YOU CHECK OUT. I'VE ALREADY BEEN SACKED TOO MANY TIMES THIS SEASON."

"I GUESS IN THIS INSTANCE **TRASH TALK** IS EXPECTED."

"WATCH THIS QUARTERBACK, HIS FATHER WAS A BOOTLEGGER."

87

"DAD, I PROMISED I WOULD TAKE YOU TO A SUPER BOWL."

"Well, the coach said I had to master the Art of Scrambling."

"NO, I'M NOT INJURED BUT I'M HAVING TROUBLE HANDLING THE CRITICISM."

NCAA OFFICIALS ROOM

"How about a new Bowl game and we'll call it the 'FISH BOWL'. The colleges won't get paid but they'll play just for the HALIBUT."

"Darn it! Here we are playing
Catch up football again".

"It's like I said, Incredible
reception, don't you agree?"

The 'Pros and Cons' of Football

"I DON'T KNOW A THING ABOUT FOOTBALL. I JUST CAME HERE BECAUSE I KEPT READING ABOUT THE ELIGIBLE RECEIVERS DOWN FIELD."

"Thanks. I did mention I needed
a wide receiver".

99

101

ANNOUNCER: "And now the Quarterback is throwing out of the Gun!"

"I wonder why the coach is worried that I might **telegraph** my passes."

"NATURALLY, AS THE DEFENSE WE ALL PREFER *TURNOVERS*."

"Okay guys, get ready. 34, 72, 45, 50 Hike!"

BASKETBALL

"THIS MUST BE A *PUMP FAKE.*"

"The coach said, 'Now go out there and try to draw a FouL'".

"IT LOOKS AS IF THE OFFICIAL IS CALLING FOR A TECHNICAL FOWL!"

"Well, he usually pulls down twenty boards a game, so he should be good at this."

"Wow! That's really a shot from in the PAINT!"

"HE'S ALWAYS BEING CALLED FOR CHARGING."

"SMITH, JUST BE SURE YOU AREN'T CALLED FOR TRAVELING."

"AREN'T YOU WORRIED ABOUT TOO MANY DOUBLE DRIBBLE CALLS?"

"DID YOU SEE THE PICK OF THE LITTER?"

"The coach says we've gotta take the air out of the ball to beat this team".

"I WISH I COULD CONVINCE RALPH THAT HE'S NOT A GUARD."

"Well, You can see from our recruiting this year, that the coach is interested in providing DOUBLE COVERAGE."

121

A TIE GAME

Truly a Cinderella Team

THE SKY ISN'T FALLING BUT IT IS RAINING BUCKETS.

"There's our star Basketball player. As always he's setting a SCREEN.

Basketball Player: "Coach, Jim just broke up with his girlfriend and I'm worried about him."

Coach: "Don't worry about Jim — he's a great rebounder."

127

"Well, Coach said to pratice our Bounce pass".

"YEAH,.. I WAS A POINT GUARD GOING ALL THE WAY BACK TO HIGH SCHOOL BASKETBALL."

"Wow, there's already a Full Court Press!"

"The coach did say he was
a great outside shooter".

"Well, Coach said I have to learn
how to hit the Bankers".

"HE'S A FORMER BASKETBALL PLAYER AND DEFINITELY AN EXCELLENT HIGH POSTMAN."

"That's not the kind of free throw I'm awarding you."

BULL MARKET

"I SHOULD HAVE KNOWN. HE WORKS AS A BRICK LAYER DURING THE SUMMER."

GOLF

"No, I Asked For a Sand Wedge."

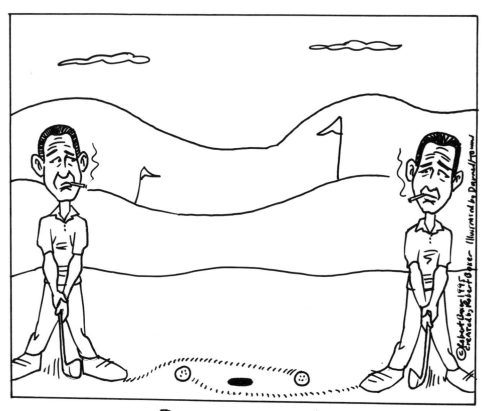

DOUBLE BOGEY

144

"I BET THEY'RE ALL SLICERS."

"WELL, I DIDN'T EXPECT HER TO BE A HOOKER."

2 THREE PUTTS

"He's working on anything that will improve his lie".

TALES FROM THE VIENNA WOODS

150

151

"HE'S GREAT AT BLASTING OUT OF A BUNKER."

"One thing about doc, he's always working on his swing."

153

"Wow, You really are trying to keep all of your IRONS in the fire, aren't you?"

"OH HONEY, WE'RE ENJOYING IT ALL THE WAY FROM THE TEE TO THE GREENS."

155

156

161

"Dr. Lance was a Professional Golfer.
He became a Surgeon so he
could for sure make all the cuts."

"THEY'RE PRACTICING FOR THE RYDER CUP."

"HERE COMES LAST YEARS WINNER WITH HIS NEW CADDY."

166

"I wonder if those are the Missing **Lynx**."

"ASK DR. PARR. HE'S A GREAT GOLFER AND ALWAYS KNOWS WHERE THE **PIN** SHOULD BE PLACED."

"HE'S BEEN LATE TO SO MANY TOURNAMENTS, MUST BE BECAUSE HE HAS A DIFFERENT **DRIVER** THAN LAST YEAR."

"TAKE ME TO YOUR LEADER."

"Take me to your leader....later."

TENNIS

THE RISE AND FALL OF THE BRITISH UMPIRE.

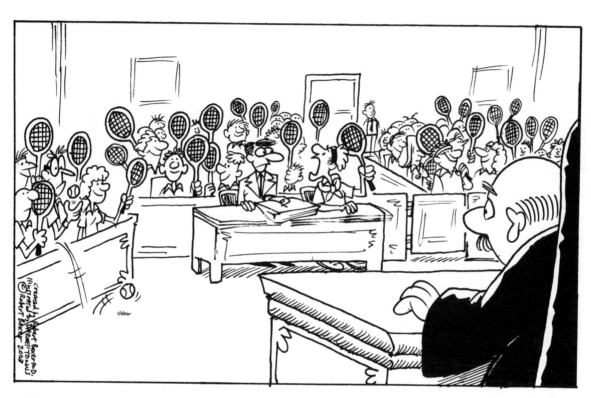

"WELL, MY COACH ALWAYS SAID I HAVE TO USE THE WHOLE COURT IN ORDER TO WIN."

"THE PROBLEM WITH YOUR STUDENTS IS THAT THEY HAVE NO GUTS."

"IF YOU KNEW WHAT HAPPENED TO HER MOTHER AND FATHER YOU'D KNOW WHY SHE DOESN'T COME UP TO THE NET."

"YEP, I'VE GOT NEW DUNLOPS"!

"OF COURSE, THEY HAVE TO USE PENN TENNIS BALLS."

"WATCH OUT FOR SUSIE AT THE NET. I'VE BEEN TO HER HOUSE FOR DINNER AND SHE'S ALWAYS POACHING."

"COACH SAID WE HAD TO LEARN TO USE THE ALLEYS."

"It pays to have relatives in High places".

"I guess we can expect to see a lot of 'Double Faults.'"

186

187

"Wow! This truly is a doubles match.!"

"YOU CARE TO VOLLEY?"

"THAT'S THE OWNER. HE'S A FORMER PROFESSIONAL TENNIS PLAYER AND HE'S ALWAYS BEEN GREAT AT **SERVING.**"

193

195

"THIS IS HOW THE COACH TRAINS THEM TO HOLD SERVE."

197

"I HAD A CHANCE TO BREAK BACK AND I TOOK IT."

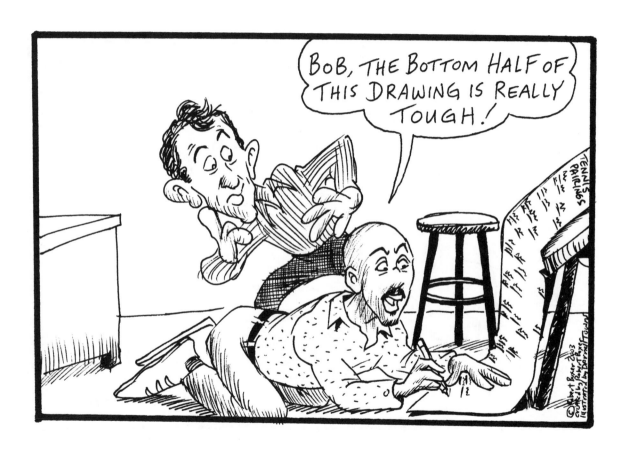

202

"I TOLD YOU I WOULD TAKE YOU TO THE SUPREME COURT."

"YES, MY RACKET IS TITANIUM. I WANTED IT TO MATCH MY DENTAL, KNEE, AND HIP IMPLANTS."

"WOULD YOU LIKE TO PLAY AUSTRALIAN DOUBLES?"

"BEST DARN TENNIS PLAYER I'VE EVER SEEN."

210

THE WOMEN'S DRAW AT THE FRENCH OPEN.

IT'S NOT OVER 'TIL IT'S OVER.

HOCKEY

"WE'RE PRACTICING IN CASE THE GAME ENDS WITH A SHOOT-OUT."

"THAT GOALIE ALWAYS FOLDS IN THE CREASE!"

"THESE ARE ALL HOCKEY PLAYERS THAT ARE PRACTICING THEIR POWER PLAY."

"WE'RE LETTING DOUG PUT THE ICING ON BECAUSE
HE'S ALWAYS CALLED FOR ICING THE PUCK."

"TAKE GOOD CARE OF GLENN, HE'S OUR BEST SAVER."

221

"WATCH OUT FOR JACQUE, HE'S BEEN INVOLVED IN ILLEGAL CHECKING."

SOCCER

THE FORCE BEHIND THE CHICAGO FIRE.

ANSWER: THE TIME OF VENUS DE MILO

"WE LOST AGAIN. I WISH JOSÉ WOULD GET HIS KICKS ON THE FIELD."

"PRETTY **HEADY** PLAY."

"I'm pretty Intellectual; I picked Soccer so I could use my Head."

229

"I'M SURE MY SON WILL BE GREAT WITH CORNER KICKS IF ONLY YOU KNEW HOW MUCH TIME HE SPENT IN THE CORNER AS A KID."

"WELL, SHE'S A FORMER SOCCER PLAYER SO SHE'S USED TO THROWING IN A FREE KICK."

MOTOR SPORTS

"DON'T WORRY. I HAVE AN AUTO IMMUNE DISEASE."

"So, How Do You Handle Your IDLE Time?!"

241

"ISN'T THIS A GREAT RACE COURSE? YOU CAN SEE THEY REALLY PULLED OUT ALL THE STOPS."

245

"Watch this guy, he usually crashes
on the last lap".

"Honey, when your cardiologist said you needed a Pacemaker, I'm sure that he didn't mean this."

"His cars went up in Flames so much they had to Induct him into the **Hall of Flame.**"

TRACK and FIELD

251

"WATCH OUT FOR JIM. YOU CAN SEE HE'S A TWO-TIMER."

"UH-OH. I THINK I JUST SUFFERED A MARCH FRACTURE."

"Yeah doc, I've been clearing the bar consistently recently. I'm working as a bouncer".

255

© Robert Boxer 1986

Created by Robert Boxer M.D.
Illustrated by Carmill Touris

Claude's Photofinishing

FILM STORAGE

"If you knew my past athletic record, you would under-stand why I'm running a Photofinishing store."

"I've been vaulting much better ever since I bought this new pole at a clearance sale".

257

"I HATE TO SEE YOU FALLING FOR HIM. YOU'LL GET HURT. HE HAS A BAD TRACK RECORD."

A POLE VAULT.

"REMEMBER, THE CHAMPIONSHIP IS JUST A HOP, SKIP AND A JUMP AWAY."

HORSE RACING and EQUESTRIAN

"This must be the line for the Daley Double."

"Now that's what I call a real gallop poll."

"This must be a Quarterhorse."

269

"CAN YOU TELL WHO'S THE SLEEPER IN THIS RACE."

GYMNASTICS

"SHE'S A FORMER GYMNAST AND HER SPECIALTY WAS THE FLOOR EXERCISE, SO SHE SHOULD BE GOOD IN THE LAYOUT DEPARTMENT."

"HE USED TO BE A CHAMPION IN GYMNASTICS SO HE'S REALLY GOOD WITH **RINGS.**"

"COACH PICKED VALERIE BECAUSE HE WAS TOLD SHE HAS A SPLIT PERSONALITY."

"Valerie always tries to eat a
well-balanced breakfast."

"OH, I KNEW HE WAS A GYMNAST, BUT I DIDN'T REALIZE THAT HIS SPECIALTY WAS THE **POMMEL HORSE.**"

SWIMMIMG, DIVING
and WATER SPORTS

"I see Coach Smith has put in all of his subs".

"Joe's a diving champion so it's important not to make a big splash."

"JUST BECAUSE YOU'RE A CHAMPION DIVER DOESN'T MEAN YOU HAVE TO ORDER EVERYTHING WITH A DOUBLE TWIST."

"NOW HERE'S A POLITICIAN WHO HAS NO TROUBLE ESTABLISHING A PLATFORM. HE USED TO BE A COMPETITIVE 10 METER DIVER."

"SHE WAS PREDICTED NOT TO DO WELL BECAUSE SHE WOULD NEVER GET PAST THE BUOYS."

FISHING, CAMPING and SHOOTING SPORTS

"The very thought of climbing mountains is rappelling to me."

"Well, you can't say we weren't warned".

FLY FISHING

"I TOLD YOU IT WAS EASY TO GET HOOKED ON FISHING."

"IS ANYONE TIRED? YA WANNA TAKE A BREAK?"
SPEAK NOW OR FOREVER HOLD YOUR PIECE!"

"I always wanted to watch **Shooting stars**."

302

"Is This the Gun Lobby I Keep Reading About?"

304

306

"HONEY, FOR SURE I'M
GOING TO HIT THE TARGET."

"WE KNEW WE WOULD FIND YOU UP HERE MAKING ROUNDS."

"MY CAR BROKE DOWN OUTSIDE. DO YOU HAVE ANY STARTER PISTOLS?"

312

"HAVE YOU MET MY STOCK TRADER?"

"OOPS! I GUESS THIS ISN'T EXACTLY THE TYPE OF BASS CAMP THAT WE INTENDED TO BRING SEYMOUR TO."

OTHER SPORTS

TOUCHÉ!

TOUPÉE!

317

"You did tell me to call a fencer, didn't you?"

"Are you two applying for DUEL citizenship?"

"Some guys get all the BREAKS."

320

ANNOUNCER: "THIS IS DENVER'S SPORTS CHANNEL BRINGING YOU THE ANNUAL SKI JUMPING COMPETITION. WE'LL BE INTERVIEWING A PROMINENT ORTHOPEDIC SURGEON RIGHT AFTER THIS BREAK."

"THAT CHALET IS MAINLY FOR SKIERS AND FIGURE SKATERS, THEY WANT TO GET USED TO BEING ON an EDGE."

"IF YOU'RE WONDERING WHY HE HAS THREE AXLES, YOU HAVE TO UNDERSTAND THE DRIVER IS A FIGURE SKATER."

"Wow, look at those great side-by-side FLYING CAMELS!"

"UNTIL I TOOK UP FIGURE SKATING, I THOUGHT A **SALCHOW** WAS A MIXED DRINK."

325

PAIRS SKATING

"Obviously those are factory seconds".

"THE CHAMP SERVES UP A MEAN KNOCKOUT PUNCH."

"IS THIS THE GRAND SLAM OF WRESTLING?"

"We Always were a Great **Tag Team.**"

"SHEILA'S MUCH BETTER AT ROOFING EVER SINCE SHE'S HAD SHINGLES."

"SHE'S THE ONLY REAL SETTER ON THE TEAM."

A VICIOUS CYCLE.

"So that's how Jim picks up his spares".

"We know you're the bull fighter's girlfriend and we love your outfit, but don't you worry that he'll think you're trying to gore his ox?"

"HEY BUDDY, COULD YOU GIVE ME A SPOT?"

338

"I brought this for those interested in more definition."

343

COMBINATION SPORTS

347

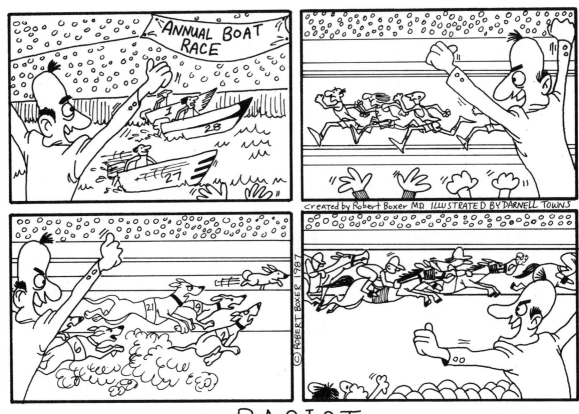

RACIST

TWO SPORTS WHERE IT IS IMPORTANT TO KNOW HOW AND WHERE TO PUT THE SHOT

"AT LEAST TODAY I HIT MORE TRIPLES THAN YOU."

351

SOME DAYS IT'S DIFFICULT TO GET THE BALL CLOSE TO THE PIN.

NOTHING BUT NET.

FANTASTIC TACKLE.

CHEAP SHOT

357

DIAMOND IN THE ROUGH.

"HE'S A FORMER GOLFER. HE'S NOT USED TO GOING MORE THAN FOUR ROUNDS."

Win, Lose or Draw!

Acknowledgments
(The Guilty Parties)

I'm particularly indebted to my very good friends, Bill, Zehava, Eitan, and Naomi Frankel. As he did for my other books, Bill, an outstanding copyright attorney, painstakingly reviewed all these cartoons. His advice, Zehava's support, and the interest of Eitan and Naomi have been invaluable. Another good friend, Nancy Janus, was extremely helpful in reviewing all the cartoons and making constructive suggestions. Marcia Steinberg typed descriptions of most of the cartoons and helped to judge the humor and artistic presentation.

Others who have been particularly encouraging and helpful include Dr. Alon Winnie, a long-time friend. Alon reviewed a number of cartoons and made useful suggestions. I'm indebted to Linda Forman, a good friend, for her ongoing support, and her interest in sports, especially in the newly-formed Chicago Sky of the WNBA. Others who have been interested and supportive include Barbara Soibel (my daughter-in-law Lisa's mother), and friends Eric Robb, Susan Cherry, Bob White, Mike Burgh, John Bruce Yeh, Teresa Reilly, Jack Boxer, Karyn and Jeff Finesilver, Frank Hagemann, Bonnie Pick, Otto Mauer, Susan Jahnke, Tracy Anderson, Jenna Yeh, Molly Yeh, Joan and Don Shrensky, Drs. Tom Stone, Alexander Golbin and Napthali Gutstein, Sheila and Howard Pizer, Shelley and Elliott Abramson, and Jody and Joel Shinbrood.

My two adult sons, Stephen and Richard, have always shared my enthusiasm for sports. Since childhood, they have been constant companions, along with my wife Marsha, at many sporting events, including basketball, football, baseball, hockey, tennis, gymnastics, ice skating, track and field, and more.

Both Stephen and Richard have enjoyed considerable success in sports, particularly in basketball, softball, and tennis. Stephen also wrote excellent commentary on sports, especially hockey, for the University of Wisconsin student newspaper. Both of my sons participated in Little League Baseball, and a Saturday morning basketball league. My wife Marsha and I were always there to support their activities. Stephen's wife, Lisa, has a very healthy interest in sports and has often accompanied me to sporting events. In high school she participated in gymnastics and ice skating. Her brother, Randy Soibel, has always been very involved in sports, especially soccer.

Our grandchildren, Jake, Nicole, and Jordaan, are also very interested in sports. Their father, Stephen, is an excellent and dedicated coach for their teams. Seven-year-old Jake not only understands my pun humor, but enthusiastically reads the cartoons and enjoys them. It is exciting to watch him and his twin siblings play baseball, T-ball, and soccer, and participate in gymnastics.

About the Author

Dr. Robert W. Boxer, named 1993 Punster of the Year by the International Save the Pun Foundation, is a practicing allergist in suburban Chicago. Bob has created thousands of pun cartoons, many of which have been illustrated by Darnell Towns.

Bob's first book, *BOXER'S SHORTS (More Than Just a Brief Attempt at Humor)*, was published in 1988. This is the fifth book in the *BOXER'S SHORTS* series.

Bob has found that discussing sports puts many of his allergy patients, including women and children, at ease. Sports talk is also a good ice breaker in many professional and social situations. Bob has been very interested in sports all his life. As a child, he followed the Kansas City Blues, an American Association minor-league Triple A farm team of the New York Yankees.

Bob played on the Kansas City, Missouri, Southwest High School tennis team for two years. He was captain and number one singles in his senior year, and reached the finals in the Kansas City boys' singles citywide tournament. He has continued to play tennis as an adult. Bob shot on Southwest's Champion ROTC rifle team in his junior and senior year of high school and he was named to the honorable mention All-City ROTC rifle team.

Bob earned his pre-medical degree at the University of Denver, where he was a member of the ice skating club. During college, he took up golf and eventually shot in the low eighties (however that was for nine holes!). Bob attended

the International Ski Championships in Aspen, Colorado. He frequently watched the University of Denver's fledgling ice hockey team, which ultimately won a number of NCAA national championships.

At Northwestern University Medical School, Bob began to follow the Chicago Cubs and White Sox. Over the years he has attended many Chicago area college and professional football and basketball games. He is a fan of the Chicago White Sox, Cubs, Bears, Bulls, Blackhawks, Sky, and Northwestern Wildcats, and enjoys watching tennis, gymnastics, ice skating, boxing, and indoor track and field. He attended the Goodwill Games in Seattle, the Summer Olympics in Los Angeles and Atlanta, the World Figure Skating Championships in Cincinnati, and the 1996 Rose Bowl game between Northwestern University and the University of Southern California. Bob has watched the Olympic swimming and diving trials at Chicago's Portage Park Pool, horse and auto racing throughout the Chicago area including Indiana and Wisconsin, professional golf tournaments, and most recently, the Chicago Sky, the new Women's National Basketball Association team.

Bob is encouraged by the emergence over the past 25 years of women's high school, collegiate and professional sports. He is especially proud of the Northwestern University Women's LaCrosse team, which took the nation by surprise by winning the national championship in 2005 and 2006.

About the Illustrator

(by the Illustrator)

Although martial arts and soccer are considered to be two of his favorite sports, Darnell Towns is first and foremost an artist of great versatility. He can draw cartoons and kick a punching bag at the same time. Darnell has been drawing recognizable images for as long or longer than a lot of professional sports figures have been playing their favorite sport as children. As a child, he enjoyed watching sports with his father, something he still does occasionally. He would lie on his favorite spot on the living room floor directly in front of the television and draw the variety of uniforms and equipment shown on the television. Darnell and his brothers, Dr. John Towns and Robert Towns, all graduated from the School of the Art Institute of Chicago, having left a great legacy there. His brother, John, the oldest of the three, helped him cultivate his art and Darnell helped his younger brother Robert, as well. Now they feed off of each other, not to seem like cannibals, but they are all well fed.

Darnell's father, Eddie Towns and Dr. Robert Boxer, contributed greatly to Darnell's understanding of sports due to their vast knowledge. But don't count on too much. Darnell still has a difficult time trying to figure out the difference between a 3 pointer and a laser pointer. Seriously, Darnell's affiliation with Dr. Boxer has been an experience, not to mention quite restful because Darnell dozes a lot when Dr. Boxer reads off his variety of puns.

Darnell has a series of comic books and comic strips coming out soon in addition to the fantastic BOXER'S SHORT series.

List of Cartoons

BASEBALL

3. To Err is Human
4. Sox Playing the Orioles
5. Spring Training
6. Relief Pitcher From the Bullpen
7. Swing and a Miss
8. Tu Tu Pitch
9. Cardinal Sin
10. Hit and Run
11. Full Counts
12. Perfect Pitch
13. Abraham Will Sacrifice
14. A Fowl Tip
15. A Game of Inches
16. Infield Fly Rule
17. Bringing in a Relief Pitcher
18. Goldberg To Run for Mayer
19. Trouble With High Pitches
20. Naming Your Son Homer
21. Clothesline Single
22. Could Always Use Another Pitcher
23. He Plays Third Base
24. Bit By a Fungo Bat
25. Opening at First Base
26. One Ball, One Strike
27. Batman Filling in
28. Baseball Leagues That Have Gone Under
29. 20,000 Leagues Under the Sea
30. Up From the Minors
31. To Bleachers
32. Wacker Drive
33. A Fowl Ball
34. Corn on the Cob
35. Stealing Second Bass
36. Walking in Runs
37. The Ottoman Empire
38. A Catch Somewhere
39. Utility Infielder
40. Picket in This Area
41. Manage in the Minors
42. No Cards Left to Play
43. I'd Rather Fight Than Switch
44. Three Homers in Every Game
45. Illegally Parked Fans
46. Lites at Wrigley Field
47. A Hit Batter
48. Hit a Sinking Liner
49. Trimming Roster
50. Practicing Going Deep
51. Interesting Bunting
52. Nobody Will Get to First Base
53. Fast Ball
54. Top and Bottom of the Fifth
55. Braking Ball
56. Our Switch Hitter
57. Just the Fall Guy
58. Unusual Wind Up
59. Broken Bat Single
60. Great Closer

FOOTBALL

63. Fake Reverse
64. Hip Pointer
65. Pulling Guard
66. Nickel Back
67. Quarterback Sneak
68. Slot Receiver
69. Quarterback Draw
70. Draw Other Team Off Sides
71. Crossing Pattern

368

147. Three Putts
148. Improve His Lie
149. Vienna Woods
150. Up Periscope
151. Up To Par
152. Blasting Out of Bunker
153. Working On His Swing
154. Irons In the Fire
155. Tee to the Greens
156. Two Shot Lead
157. Bogeyman
158. Tee or Tea Time?
159. Wrong Score
160. Chip Off the Old Block
161. New Iron
162. Birdie and Eagle
163. Make All the Cuts
164. The Ryder Cup
165. New Caddy
166. Any of Your Lip
167. Missing Lynx
168. Ask Dr. Parr
169. Different Driver
170. Take Me To Your Leader
171. To Your Leader . . . Later

TENNIS
175. British Umpire
176. Allergic to Shrimps
177. Use the Whole Court
178. Have No Guts
179. Come Up To the Net
180. New Dunlops
181. Penn Tennis Balls
182. Always Poaching
183. Use the Alleys
184. Relatives In High Places
185. Double Faults
186. Crab to Lobster
187. No Strings Attached
188. Doubles Match
189. The First Serve
190. Choking At End of Match
191. Care to Volley?
192. Great At Serving
193. No Fault Insurance
194. Playing With Authority
195. Sharpness at the End of a Match is Important
196. Seeds in This Tournament
197. Hold Serve
198. Break Back

199. Closing the School
200. Start With a Double Fault
201. Not Enough Guts
202. Tough Bottom Half of Drawing
203. Don't Have Any Aces
204. Supreme Court
205. Back Handed Compliment
206. Titanium
207. Australian Doubles
208. Really Great Server
209. Looking for a Prince
210. Best Darn Tennis Player
211. The Women's Draw
212. Not Over Until It's Over

HOCKEY
215. Ends With a Shoot Out
216. Folds In the Crease
217. Power Play
218. Icing the Puck
219. Our Best Saver
220. Cheap Skates
221. Slapstick Humor
222. Illegal Checking

311. Starter Pistols
312. Sights Too High
313. Stock Trader
314. Bring Seymour To Bass Camp

OTHER SPORTS
317. Touche' Toupee'
318. Call a Fencer
319. Duel Citizenship
320. Get All the Breaks
321. Right After This Break
322. Being On An Edge
323. Triple Axle
324. Flying Camels
325. Salchow
326. Pairs Skating
327. Factory Seconds
328. Mean Knockout Punch
329. Grand Slam of Wrestling
330. Great Tag Team
331. Better Roofer Since Shingles
332. Only Real Setter
333. Vicious Cycle
334. Pick Up Spares
335. Beau in Arrow
336. Gore His Ox
337. Give Me a Spot
338. Mussel Bound
339. More Definition
340. Crew Cuts
341. Archer Avenue Parade
342. The Next Olympics
343. Parting Shot

COMBINATION SPORTS
347. Is the Safety On?
348. Racist
349. Pro-Bowler
350. Put the Shot
351. More Triples
352. Ball Close To Pin
353. Nothing But Net
354. Fantastic Tackle
355. Cheap Shot
356. Turkey
357. Guard For Football and Basketball
358. Diamond In the Rough
359. Bowling Green
360. Former Golfer
361. Luck of the Draw
362. Win, Lose or Draw

Book Order Form

TITLE	QUANTITY	PRICE*	IL RESIDENTS STATE SALES TAX	AMOUNT
Boxer Shorts 5: The Sports Book	_____	$19.95 ea.	$1.60 ea.	_____
Boxer Shorts 4: The Music Book	_____	$14.95 ea.	$1.20 ea.	_____
Boxer Shorts 3: The Medical Version	_____	$12.95 ea.	$1.04 ea.	_____
Boxer Shorts: Round 2	_____	$9.95 ea.	$0.80 ea.	_____
Boxer Shorts: More Than Just a Brief Attempt at Humor	_____	$7.95 ea.	$0.64 ea.	_____
Set of all five books in the series, if available		$54.95	$5.00	_____
			Subtotal	_____
Shipping & handling, $3.95. 2 or more books, $5.95.			S&H	_____
			TOTAL	_____

Name_____

Address_____

City_____

State_____ Zip _____

Country_____

Check your local bookstore, visit our Web site at www.boxers-shorts.com, or order with this form.

If ordering with this form, send check or money order made payable to Punchline Press, Box 308, Wilmette, IL 60091

(Prices subject to change without notice.)
Order subject to availability. Please allow four–six weeks for delivery. All amounts are in U.S. Dollars.

Punchline Press™ books are available at quantity discounts with bulk purchase for educational, business, or sales promotional use. For information, please write to Special Orders Dept. Punchline Press, Box 308, Wilmette, IL 60091, or visit our Web site at www.boxers-shorts.com

Satisfaction Guaranteed—Books in perfect condition (original) may be returned within six months for complete refund.